AF585209

Australian States *and Territories*

AUSTRALIAN CAPITAL TERRITORY

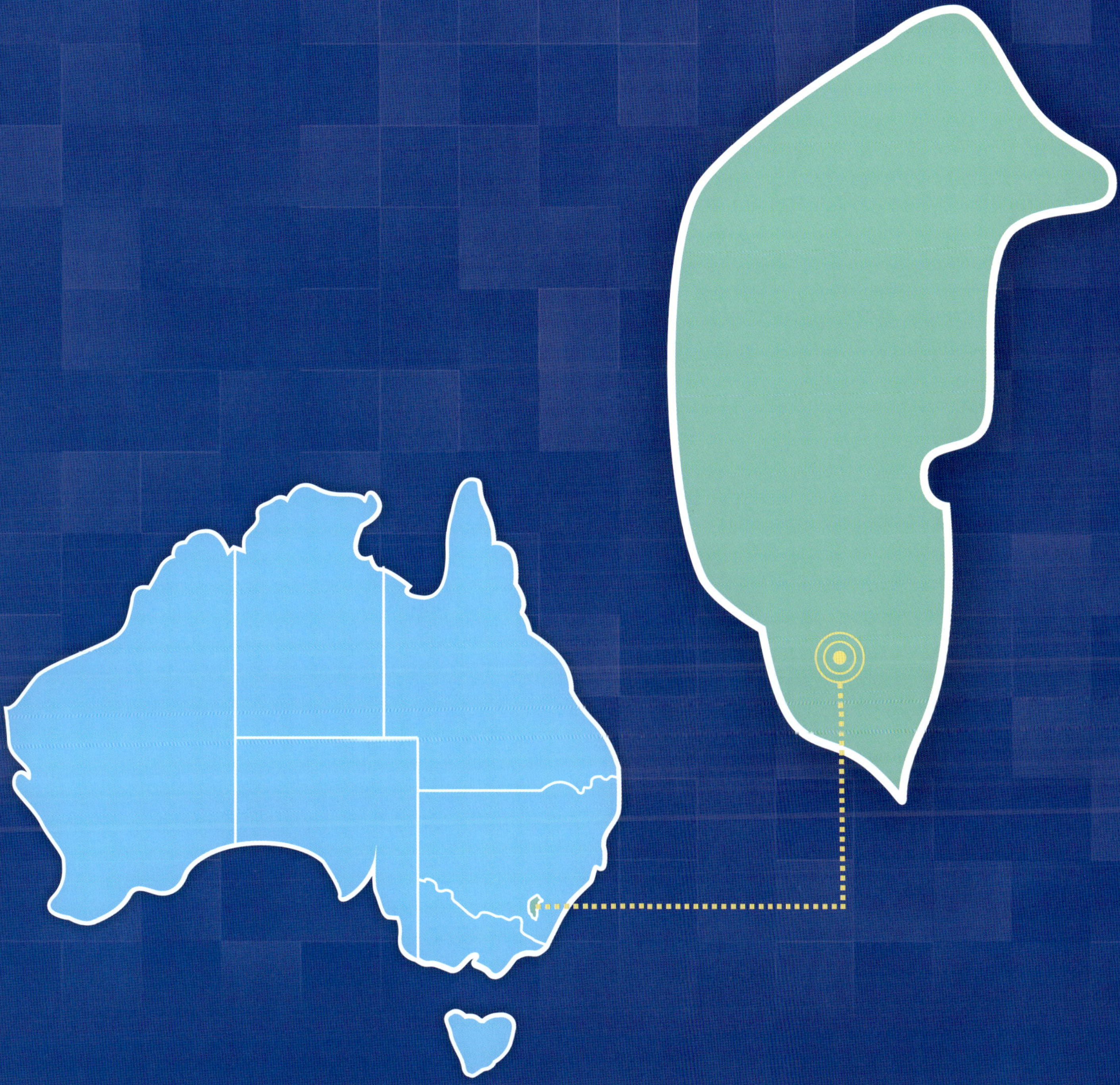

Linsie Tan

Redback Publishing
PO Box 357 Frenchs Forest NSW 2086
Australia

ISBN 978-0-9946247-0-3

First published 2017
Reprinted 2018

Author: Linsie Tan
Editor: Jane Hinchey
Original illustrations © Redback Publishing 2017
Originated by Redback Publishing
Printed and bound in China by Leo Paper

Acknowledgements
We would like to thank the following for permission to reproduce photographs: NathanHurst at the English language Wikipedia, Willem van Aken, Carl Davies, Claudio Bertoloni / Shutterstock.com, Nick-D, Bidgee, Dixson Library, State Library of NSW, Tooykrub / Shutterstock.com, Ryszard Stelmachowicz / Shutterstock.com, Nadezda Zavitaeva / Shutterstock.com, Andy Lidstone / Shutterstock.com, Lefteris Papaulakis / Shutterstock.com, National Library of Australia - Portrait of Rosemary Follett, Chief Minister for the A.C.T, 1994, Andrew Stawowczyk, PIC NL37528, Nick-D, tristan tan / Shutterstock.com, STRINGER Image / Shutterstock.com, Eva Rinaldi, National Library of Australia - Portrait of A.T. Shakespeare of the Canberra Times, L.J. Dwyer, PIC Box PIC/6201, Richard Gifford, Grahamec, Squiresy92. P6 NAA: A3560, 4317 Sydney building Northbourne Avenue and motor cars from colonades of Melbourne building.

Cataloguing-in-Publication details are available from the National Library of Australia

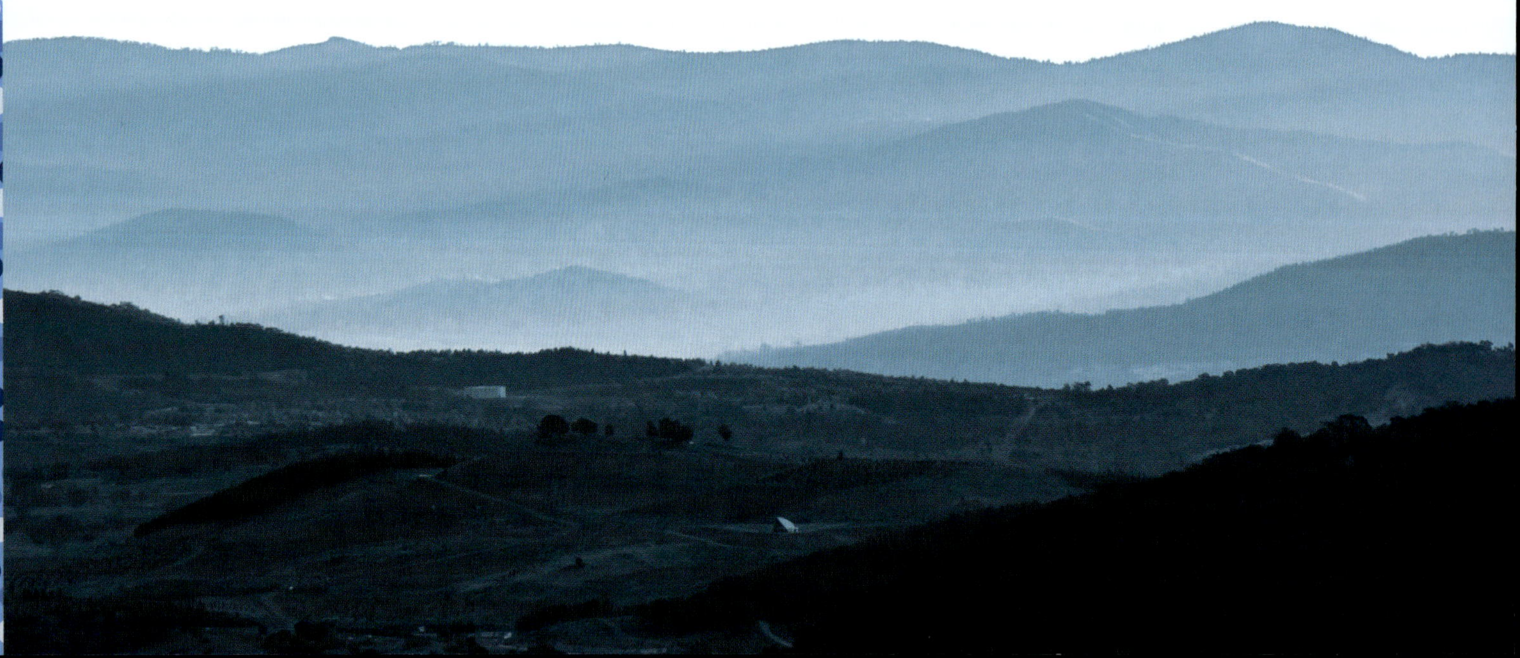

CONTENTS

Some words are shown in red, **like this**.
You can find out what they mean by
looking in the glossary.

Canberra

Canberra is Australia's capital city. It is located within the Australian Capital Territory, which is an area surrounded by the state of New South Wales.

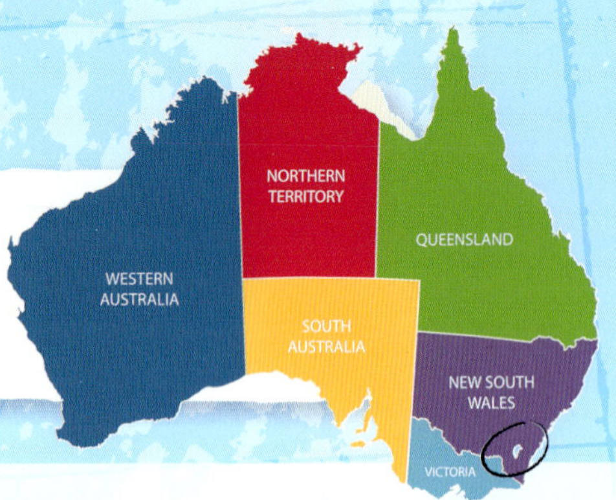

History of Canberra

The first European explorers came through the area in the early 1820s, and Joshua John Moore was already running livestock there by 1823. He named his property Canberry.

When the Commonwealth of Australia was created on 1st January 1901, the new nation did not have a capital city and the ACT did not exist. The first Australian Parliament met in Melbourne and began to investigate possible sites for the new capital city.

Naming the Capital City

The name of the new capital city was kept a secret until Lady Denman, wife of the Governor General, announced it at the foundation ceremony on 12th March 1913. Taking a card from a golden box, she read the name to the waiting crowds. The meaning of the word Canberra is not certain, but it is possibly an Aboriginal word for 'meeting place'.

FAST FACT

The new capital city had to be located at least 160 km away from Sydney, because of the rivalry that existed between Melbourne and Sydney

Walter Burley Griffin (1876 - 1937)

An international design competition was held in 1911 to create a plan for the new capital city. The winner was Walter Burley Griffin, an American architect. His designs were influenced by the Garden City style of town design which was popular at the time. His wife, Marion Mahony Griffin, created the drawings for her husband's designs. The ACT's first newspaper complained in 1924 that Griffin's designs did not include streets or localities named after any of the area's explorers or pioneers.

Griffin's early career in the United States included a period spent working with the renowned architect Frank Lloyd Wright. After moving to Australia, Griffin worked on many projects besides the planning of Canberra, including house designs, town plans and civic buildings and structures. His designs for the NSW towns of Leeton and Griffith both show the same circular themes that he used for Canberra.

Griffin died in Lucknow, India, where he was working on plans for public and private buildings. Although he faced criticism during his lifetime for the extravagance of his designs for Canberra, later generations of Australians admire the breadth and beauty of his ideas for the nation's capital city.

The Design for Canberra

Walter Burley Griffin's design planned for future growth, with wide roads and room for expanding suburbs. He separated the town centre and government precinct, and included a large man-made lake. The designs of the layout are geometric, with circular roads, long avenues and precincts bounded with triangular and hexagonal shapes. The Parliamentary Triangle places Parliament House at the top of a large triangle of roads which extend across Lake Burley Griffin.

Lake Burley Griffin

This lake was a part of Griffin's design, but it was not created until 1963, after a dam was constructed on the Molonglo River to provide the water.

Parliament House

Griffin planned for Parliament House to stand just below Capital Hill, but his exact designs were not followed. On top of the hill where Parliament House now stands, Griffin had imagined a stepped pyramid, which was to be a ceremonial venue rather than a place of government.

Open Space

Open space was a very important part of Griffin's design for Canberra. He included formal parks, extensive garden areas around public buildings and also allowed for natural bushland to be retained. Black Mountain and Mount Ainslie are two areas where Canberrans can enjoy bushwalking and the natural environment.

WORD FILE

precinct - an area within a city

Canberra Grows Slowly

Set amidst sheep farms, Australia's capital city developed very slowly. The two World Wars and the Great Depression of the 1930s hampered the growth of the new city.

In the 1950s, Prime Minister Menzies transferred more of the public service departments from Melbourne to Canberra. Embassies for other nations relocated to Canberra and, by the 1960s, Canberra had become a city surrounded by growing suburbs.

Civic

From the 1920s to the 1940s, Canberra's shopping and business centre developed based on two colonnaded buildings on Northbourne Avenue. They were named the Sydney Building and the Melbourne Building. There were few other shops in Canberra apart from the ones in these buildings, and many locals visited Queanbeyan for their shopping needs. In 1963, the Monaro Mall was opened. It was the first enclosed, multi-level shopping centre anywhere in Australia.

Walter Burley Griffin had planned for the shopping precinct to be called Civic Centre, but the shortened name Civic became the term used by locals.

SISTER CITIES

Sister City programs encourage interactions that promote business and cultural ties. Canberra's Sister Cities are:

- **Nara in Japan**
- **Beijing in China**

Sydney Building across Northbourne Avenue from the colonnades of the Melbourne Building, Civic Centre, 1932

The Australian Government

THE AUSTRALIAN PARLIAMENT

Australia is a democracy in which citizens vote for the Senators and Members of Parliament. Australia is also a constitutional monarchy, in which Queen Elizabeth II is represented locally by the Governor General.

The Australian Parliament has a bicameral system, with two houses that sit in Parliament House in Canberra.

The Senate - 76 Senators

The House of Representatives - 150 Members

Lower house of the bicameral parliament

WORD FILE

bicameral - a government having two houses or sections

Upper house of the bicameral parliament

THE AUSTRALIAN CONSTITUTION

The Australian Constitution was created by an act of the British Parliament in 1900. The role of the Constitution is to define the way the Australian government will operate. It does this by establishing the following political frameworks:

The Parliament - The legislative branch of government

The Executive Government - The Governor General, the Prime Minister and the appointed Ministers

The Judicature - The High Court and other federal courts

The States - The Constitution sets out how the powers of the states are different from those of the Commonwealth

Referendums - The Constitution can only be changed by voters at a referendum

THE HIGH COURT

The Australian Constitution provided for the creation of a High Court. The High Court originally sat in Melbourne and later in Sydney. The High Court building in Canberra opened in 1980. The first Justice of the High Court was Sir Samuel Griffith in 1903. The first woman to be appointed a Justice of the High Court was Mary Gaudron in 1987.

The Australian High Court building, beside Lake Burley Griffin

FUNCTIONS OF THE HIGH COURT INCLUDE:

- To decide on disputes between the Commonwealth and state governments
- To interpret the meaning of the Constitution
- To provide a court of appeal from the states and territories

WESTMINSTER SYSTEM

The Westminster System describes a parliamentary democracy that is based on the type of government that exists in Britain, Australia, New Zealand and Canada. The name comes from the area in London where the parliament is located.

FEATURES OF THE WESTMINSTER SYSTEM

- There is an elected lower house of parliament
- The political party receiving the highest number of votes at an election becomes the government. The party receiving the second highest number of votes becomes the opposition
- The monarch and their representative, the governor general, are advised by the head of the government
- The law courts are independent of the government

SECTIONS OF GOVERNMENT IN A WESTMINSTER SYSTEM

The Legislature or Parliament - debates and votes on laws
The Executive - ensures laws are carried out
The Judiciary - enforces and interprets the laws

THE MAGNA CARTA

The original Magna Carta, (Latin for Great Charter), dates from 1215. It is a document detailing an agreement between the King of England and his barons, setting out their basic rights and emphasising the importance of the law. It shows the first, tentative steps towards representative government.

The Magna Carta became the basis for all laws made in England, and it also influenced the creation of the Australian Constitution in 1901. A copy of the Magna Carta from 1297 is on display at Parliament House in Canberra. It was acquired by the Australian Government in 1952.

Magna Carta, 1297 version

TYPES OF GOVERNMENT IN AUSTRALIA

Australians vote for three levels of government and voting is compulsory. Each level of government is responsible for different services.

Federal Government

Australian citizens over the age of 18 must vote in Federal elections.

The Federal government is responsible for defence, pensions, Medicare, universities, foreign affairs and trade, immigration, national finances, interstate roads and communication, income taxation and its distribution to the states.

State and Territory Governments

Australian citizens over the age of 18 must vote in state elections for the state in which they live.

State and territory governments are responsible for schools, hospitals, main roads and police services.

Local Governments

Australian citizens over the age of 18 must vote in local government elections for the area in which they live. Owners of land can also vote even if they are not residents, but voting for them is not compulsory, except in the City of Sydney council elections.

Local government looks after suburban roads, parks, libraries, swimming pools, local planning and building regulations and rubbish removal.

CITIZENSHIP

Australian citizens are either born in Australia or have settled from overseas and become citizens at a citizenship ceremony. At this ceremony, new citizens must take the Australian Citizenship Pledge. The first citizenship ceremony was held in Canberra in 1949.

AUSTRALIAN CITIZENSHIP PLEDGE

From this time forward, (under God),
I pledge my loyalty to Australia and its people,
whose democratic beliefs I share,
whose rights and liberties I respect, and
whose laws I will uphold and obey.

FAST FACTS

Aboriginal Australians and Citizenship

1962 - Aboriginal Australians could vote in federal elections

1967 - Aboriginal Australians were now included in the census

Australian Citizens Have Rights and Responsibilities

RIGHTS

The right to vote
The right to receive an Australian passport
The right to receive certain benefits from the Australian government

RESPONSIBILITIES

To uphold and obey the laws
To be loyal to Australia and its people
To serve in Australia's defence if necessary

Geography of the ACT

Canberra, Australia's capital city, is located in the north of the ACT. In the south is the Namadgi National Park, covering about 40 per cent of the ACT. Most of the flatter areas of the ACT have been cleared for pastures and agriculture. The hills and low mountains in the remaining areas are covered with sclerophyll forests and sub-alpine vegetation. The Murrumbidgee River and its main tributaries, the Cotter River and the Molonglo River, flow through the ACT.

Beyond the city of Canberra and its suburbs there are also a number of small villages in the ACT including Hall, Naas, Tharwa, Uriarra and Williamsdale.

PREDICT THE POPULATION

Draw a graph and use it to estimate what the population will be in 2030.

YEAR	1930	1950	1970	1990	2010	2030
POPULATION of the ACT	9,000	24,000	138,000	285,000	365,000	?

Murrumbidgee river

WEATHER

- Highest recorded temperature in Canberra 42.2 °C in 1968
- Lowest recorded temperature in Canberra −10.0 °C in 1971

WORD FILE

sclerophyll forest - forest plants having tough leaves that resist drying out
sub-alpine - at the lower regions of mountains

Aboriginal History of the ACT

Aboriginal people have lived in the ACT for at least 20,000 years. They developed a complex society and way of life, and their culture depends on having strong spiritual connections to the land.

The Ngunnawal People

Canberra and the ACT are on the traditional lands of the Ngunnawal people. Their meeting grounds were near Black Mountain and called Kamberra. The local Bogong moth feast was an annual event which drew neighbouring Aboriginal people to the area for meetings and trade.

When European settlers arrived in the ACT, they colonised areas that had been in traditional ownership for thousands of years. Sheep replaced the native food animals on the land and forests were cleared for pastures. The Ngunnawal people continued their traditional occupation of the land, but some also sought employment on local farms.

FAST FACTS

Three known language groups of the Namadgi area:

Ngunnawal
Ngarigo
Walgalu

Namadgi National Park

The Namadgi National Park was declared in 1984. In 2001, the Ngunnawal Aboriginal people were recognised as the traditional custodians and now manage the park together with the ACT government.

There are about 400 sites of Aboriginal importance in the park, including the rock art at Yankee Hat in the Gudgenby Valley. These paintings show people, animals and abstract symbols in a style that appears across the whole Southern Tablelands region.

The bushfire of 2003 destroyed large parts of the park, but also resulted in the exposure of historic Aboriginal sites that were not previously documented.

Locations of Aboriginal Heritage Sites in the ACT

The Tidbinbilla area is a valley surrounded by the Australian Alps. There is a sacred site nearby where boys' initiation ceremonies were held. Rock shelters, rock art and artefacts have been found throughout Tidbinbilla, and there is a quarry where the stone for tools was mined. A walking trail has been created so that people today can find the Birrigai Rock Shelter, which is one of the oldest and most spectacular rock shelters in the ACT.

At Red Hill there was an ochre quarry where the ingredients for paint were mined. Ochre produced a ceremonial paint used to decorate the body and possessions, and to create art on rock walls.

The small town of Tharwa is part of a Dreaming path where Ngunnawal ancestors travelled the land.

There are scarred trees throughout the ACT. These are evidence of Aboriginal occupation of the land. The bark was peeled from the trees to build canoes and shelters, or for making containers and shields.

The placement of stones and rocks in circles and lines suggests that the locations were used for ceremonial or meeting purposes. Stones placed in an upright position have also been found in the ACT.

Boulders near Tidbinbilla rock shelter

FAST FACT

Aboriginal heritage sites are still being found in the ACT. Any person who thinks they have found such a site must report it to the Heritage Unit of the ACT government.

WORD FILE

colonise - to settle in a new land and impose a new culture on the people living there
traditional ownership - the Aboriginal land ownership system

Settlement of the ACT

The area which is now the site of Canberra and the ACT was once a part of the colony of New South Wales.

Timeline of Settlement in the ACT

BEFORE 1788 The Ngunnawal people were the traditional custodians of the land.

1788 Governor Phillip founded the colony of New South Wales.

1802 to 1821 Charles Throsby and his nephew, along with Joseph Wild and James Vaughan, explored the area and found the Limestone Plains, Lake George, the Molonglo River and the Murrumbidgee River. They reported that the plains would provide good pastures for sheep and cattle.

1823 Captain Mark Currie explored the Tuggeranong area and called it Isabella's Plain.

1823 to 1830 Large properties were established on the land now occupied by Canberra. They included Canberry, Springbank, Duntroon and Yarralumla.

1862 Tharwa became the first official settlement in the area.

EARLY 1900 Settlers relied on Queanbeyan as the nearest town.

1909 Charles Scrivener camped on Kurrajong Hill, which later became Capital Hill and the site of Parliament House. Scrivener surveyed the area and made recommendations to the government on where the nation's capital should be located.

1911 NSW transferred the land for the ACT to the Commonwealth.

1913 Canberra was founded.

Oldest Church

St John the Baptist Church in Reid is the ACT's oldest church, dating from 1845. The first tower had to be taken down when it developed a dangerous lean. The second tower was designed by colonial architect Edmund Blacket, who was also responsible for the imposing sandstone buildings of the University of Sydney.

The earliest school in the area operated from St John's schoolhouse, which is now a museum. The churchyard was the first cemetery for Canberra and burials date from 1844.

Left: Part of the graveyard and lawns of St John's Church

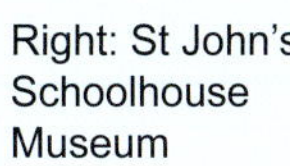

Right: St John's Schoolhouse Museum

Far right: St John's Church

Bushrangers

The remote country around the site of Canberra encouraged bushrangers to prey on settlers and travellers. Local forests and caves provided perfect bushranger hideouts.

Bushrangers who roamed the region long before it became known as Canberra included Ben Hall, William Westwood and the notorious Clarke gang.

John Tennant

John Tennant was a bushranger who terrorised locals in the1820s. Nicknamed the Terror of Argyle, Tennant was captured at Tuggeranong by James Ainslie, an employee of the man who owned the Duntroon property. Tennant was hung and, despite his criminal activities, Mount Tennent was probably named after him, although the spelling of the name is different. There is a legend in the area around Tharwa that Tennant's hoard of stolen goods is still hidden somewhere in the hills.

Clarke brothers

Transport in the ACT

Pre-Colonial Transport

The first methods of transport used by Aboriginal people in Australia were walking and paddling canoes. Canoes were made of bark or from hollowed out logs, and they were used for fishing and to cross rivers. 'Canoe trees' are important reminders of this early technology.

Fishing in a bark canoe

Roads

Roads in the ACT were dirt tracks in the colonial era, and agricultural produce was often transported in carts pulled by bullocks.

Settlers walked when travelling, or rode horses or in carriages or carts if they could afford them.

The layout of the circular roads, roundabouts and long avenues in the centre of Canberra was designed by Walter Burley Griffin.

Sea Port at Jervis Bay

Land for the ACT was transferred from the NSW government in 1911. A few years later, Jervis Bay was also made a Commonwealth territory, under the control of the ACT. Even though the two areas have no physical connection, Jervis Bay was supposed to provide Canberra with access to a sea port. A railway linking the two areas was planned in 1914 but never built. The Booderee National Park and the naval base HMAS Creswell are located at Jervis Bay.

Air Transport

RAAF Base Fairbairn

The RAAF had a permanent airbase in Canberra from 1940 to 2004. It was originally named RAAF Station Canberra, but was renamed when crew and passengers, including the Air Minister James Fairbairn, were killed when their aircraft crashed into a hill near the base in 1940. The RAAF used the base during the Second World War to launch anti-submarine patrols and for operations involving the Netherlands Air Force. Aircraft from the base were sent out to search for escapees when there was a mass breakout from the Cowra prisoner of war camp.

Canberra Airport

Canberra's first airport in the 1920s was a small landing strip with no facilities. Sheep grazed on the airfield when no flights were due to arrive.

On 21st September 2016, Canberra Airport celebrated the commencement of an international service linking Singapore, Canberra and New Zealand. The passengers were handed floral bouquets and the Singapore Airlines plane was greeted with a water salute sprayed from the airport's fire vehicles.

Bus Services

Since there are no railway or tram services operating within the ACT, buses, long distance coaches and private vehicles are the main means of transport. The first bus services began running in 1926.

Railway

In 1887, the railway in NSW was extended to Queanbeyan. Residents of the ACT relied on Queanbeyan for their rail connection to Sydney up until 1914, when the first steam train to the ACT began operations. That train is now in the Canberra Railway Museum.

Walter Burley Griffin's plan involved railway lines linking all of Canberra. The only part of his plan to be built is the line from Queanbeyan in NSW to Kingston, which is Canberra's only railway station, built in 1924.

Industries and Agriculture in the ACT

Government

The business of running a government is the main industry in the ACT. Governments require administrative services and their employees need shops, schools, health care and places to live.

Not only is the Australian Parliament located in the ACT, but the territory also has its own government, which combines the roles of both a state and local government. As a result, computers and electronic equipment are the highest value imports into the ACT.

Tourism

Although the ACT and Canberra were once dusty sheep farms, there are now many attractions to interest tourists. These include Parliament House, the many museums and galleries, the national parks and Lake Burley Griffin.

The first visitor hotels in Canberra were the Hotel Canberra and the Hotel Kurrajong, both built in the 1920s. Their customers were mostly politicians and others involved in government. There are now many hotels of international standard in Canberra.

The 2020 Tourism Strategy, compiled by the ACT government, sets the objectives for increasing tourism and its contribution to the economy of the ACT.

School Excursions

Every year, thousands of students from around Australia visit Canberra on school excursions. All the main sites of government provide educational programs for visiting students, and many offer interactive experiences to help children understand the way the Australian Parliament functions.

Transport and tour operators produce special packages for school excursion students and their teachers, and accommodation ranges from hotels to hostels and bush cabins.

Providing facilities for school excursions to Canberra is an important industry which employs many people in the ACT and contributes to the economy. In 1999, a group of businesses involved in this industry formed the National Capital Educational Tourism Project. The aim of this group is to make Canberra the top educational tourism destination in Australia.

Floriade

Floriade is an annual spring flower festival that attracts visitors from Australia and overseas. The first Floriade was held in 1988. Since then, the festival has grown to become one of the ACT's largest tourist attractions.

Exports

The ACT was created to be a seat for the government of Australia, but it also has an export industry for the following specialised products:

- Coins produced at the Royal Australian Mint
- Medical electronic equipment
- Lime, cement & construction materials

Agriculture

There is more to the ACT than just the business of government. It also supports a varied agricultural industry which supplies produce for local and other consumers.

Crops, Horticulture and Livestock in the ACT
fruit, vegetables, beef, pork, poultry, wheat, flowers

FAST FACTS

The Royal Australian Mint has made coins for:

- **Australia**
- **The Solomon Islands**
- **Vanuatu**
- **Tonga**
- **The Cook Islands**
- **Samoa**

Environment and Sustainability in the ACT

Sustainable practices require a balance between using the land and waterways for development and keeping areas as regions of natural beauty.

RESOURCES	HOW WE CAN LOOK AFTER THEM
SOIL	Correct use of fertilisers and avoiding soil erosion
WATER	Keeping water supplies unpolluted
NATIVE PLANTS	Avoid complete clearing of areas for pastures
NATIVE ANIMALS	Keep some areas of natural bushland for food and shelter
AIR QUALITY	Avoid polluting the air through poor industrial practices

Water

Water Resources in the ACT

The ACT is in the Murrumbidgee River Catchment, which connects with the Murray-Darling river system. This means that all water usage and runoff needs to be carefully controlled. Some of these control measures include:

- Slowing down water runoff into stormwater drains
- Reducing pollutants and sediments in the runoff
- Water usage reduction measures in new residential developments

About 85 per cent of Canberra's water supply comes from the Namadgi National Park catchment. There are four dams supplying water to Canberra. They are the Corin Dam, Bendora Dam, Cotter Dam and Googong Dam.

Water Usage at Floriade, Canberra's Floral Festival

- Water for Floriade is drawn from Lake Burley Griffiin
- Recycling and water conservation are encouraged
- Commonwealth Park is restored after the event is over using drought-tolerant grasses

WORD FILE

sustainability - ability of the environment to be used without being destroyed

Renewable Energy

The ACT receives 99 per cent of its electricity supply from outside the territory, but the government is seeking to increase its use of renewable energy sources to include wind and solar.

Plants and Animals

Rare and threatened plants, animals, invertebrates and aquatic wildlife are protected in the ACT.

Northern Corroboree Frogs

This threatened species lives in mossy, alpine areas in the Brindabella and Bimberi Ranges of the ACT. The frog is 2-3 cm long and there may be only about fifty left in the wild in the ACT. Its numbers declined due to the 2003 bushfires, and it also suffers from infection by a fungal disease. A captive breeding program is attempting to save the Northern Corroboree Frog from extinction.

Bushfires

Bushfires have been a threat to the ACT since it was first founded.

The 2003 Bushfires

In 2003, bushfires destroyed the Mount Stromlo Observatory and damaged hundreds of houses in the outer suburbs of Canberra. These fires resulted in an added problem when they burnt bush in the ACT's water catchment area. This affected the water runoff and therefore Canberra's water supply.

The ACT Rural Fire Service

The ACT Rural Fire Service fights bush and grass fires that occur within rural areas of the ACT. The service operates using both volunteers and employees. They fight bushfires, conduct hazard reduction burning and advise the public on bushfire safety measures.

Horses and Bushfires

Canberra has a very high number of horse owners. During the 2003 bushfires, horses and their owners were in danger and some owners risked their lives to save their animals. The ACT Rural Fire Service recognised that looking after their horses was a priority for many owners in the ACT, so it has published a study on the safe evacuation of people and horses during a bushfire.

Fires and the Australian Bush

Fire has played a role in the evolution of vegetation in the Australian bush. Some plants require the heat of a bushfire before their seedpods will open. The burning of the forest canopy, which increases the amount of light that reaches the ground, and the layer of ash after a bushfire, can both contribute to the germination and growth of seeds.

Government of the ACT

Rosemary Follett

The Australian Capital Territory has its own unicameral government. It is the only government in Australia to have both territory and local responsibilities. When the ACT was created in 1911, residents lost the right to vote in state and local elections. They did not regain full local voting rights until 1989, when the ACT Legislative Assembly was formed.

The head of government in the ACT is called the Chief Minister. The first Chief Minister was Rosemary Follett, who was also the first woman to become head of any Australian government.

Timeline for Government of the ACT

1911 An area called the Federal Capital Territory (FCT) was administered by the Federal Minister for Territories.

1938 The FCT was renamed the Australian Capital Territory (ACT).

1920 - 1974 Local committees were appointed to advise the Minister on behalf of the residents.

1963 The first sitting of the Supreme Court of the ACT.

Supreme Court ACT

1974 Residents elected a Legislative Assembly but the Minister still had the right to overrule its decisions.

1989 The ACT became self governing and the first meeting of its independent Legislative Assembly was held.

Electorates for the ACT Legislative Assembly

Brindabella
Ginninderra
Kurrajong
Murrumbidgee
Yerrabi

The 2016 election increased the number of members from 17 to 25, with 5 for each of the electorates.

FAST FACT

The carpet in the Legislative Assembly is decorated with the Royal Bluebell, the floral emblem of the ACT.

Twinning Arrangement With Kiribati

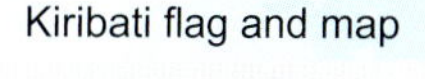
Kiribati flag and map

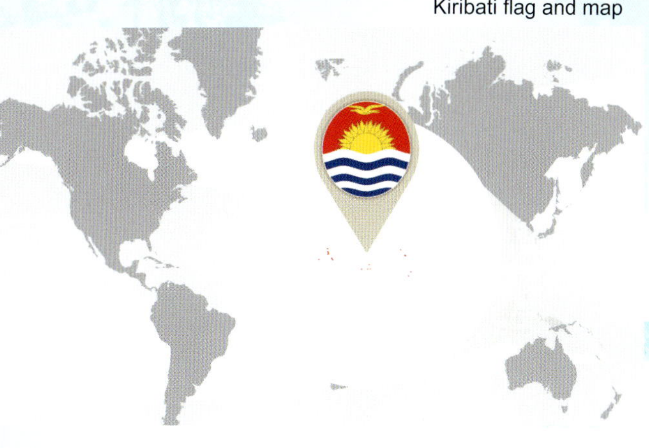

Kiriabti is a small nation in the Pacific Ocean at the Equator. The Legislative Assembly of the ACT has a Twinning Arrangement with the Parliament of Kiribati. Twinning provides an opportunity for exchanges of parliamentary information and advice. The first meetings between the ACT and Kiribati were held in 2008.

ACT Legislative Assembly Building

The first meetings of the ACT Legislative Assembly were held in temporary premises. In 1994, the government moved to renovated premises in the South Building on Civic Square.

The copper sculpture in front of the ACT Legislative Assembly building was created by artist Tom Bass in 1961. It represents Ethos and is a symbol of pride in the community.

WORD FILE

unicameral - a government having one house or section

Notable People from the ACT

ACT Honour Walk

The ACT Honour Walk is in Ainslie Place, between London Circuit and the Canberra Times Fountain. Plaques have been laid into a pathway since 2005 to recognise people and groups whose contributions to the ACT have been significant.

William Farrer (1845 – 1906) Farrer's experiments into breeding new strains of rust resistant wheat provided colonial Australia with products that would grow well in the local conditions and that could be exported to the rest of the world. Before his scientific work produced new resistant forms of wheat, local growers had experienced a disastrous crop that had been ruined by disease. Farrer conducted his experiments at Lambrigg, his property near Tharwa in the ACT.

Nick Kyrgios (1985 –) Born in Canberra, Nick Kyrgios is a high profile tennis player who has been ranked number one in Australia. He is also a supporter of many charities. Kyrgios represented the ACT in basketball before deciding to concentrate on his tennis career.

Sigrid Thornton (1959 –) Sigrid Thornton is an actress who was born in Canberra. She has appeared in many iconic film, television and theatre productions. She also works in administrative roles to further the dramatic arts industry in Australia.

Charles Throsby (1777 – 1828) Charles Throsby was the first European to explore the ACT area. In expeditions from 1802 to 1821, Charles Throsby and his nephew, along with Joseph Wild and James Vaughan, found the Limestone Plains, Lake George, the Molonglo River and the Murrumbidgee River. They reported that the plains would provide good pastures for sheep and cattle, which encouraged others to settle there.

Joshua John Moore (1790 – 1864) Between 1824 and 1826, Moore developed his property called Canberry. He employed a manager who, with the help of convict labourers, built huts, stockyards and fences. In 1843, Moore sold the property and the new owner called it Acton. Parts of Civic and the Australian National University are located on this land.

Thomas Shakespeare (1873 – 1938) Thomas Shakespeare published the first issue of the Canberra Times in 1926, and his family continued to manage it until its sale in 1964. The newspaper operated from offices that Shakespeare acquired in 1924, when the first leases for commercial buildings in Canberra were made available to the public.

James Ainslie (1787 – 1844) In 1825, James Ainslie drove a flock of sheep owned by Robert Campbell into the Limestone Plains area and settled on the property called Duntroon. After a disagreement with Campbell, Ainslie returned to Scotland. Mount Ainslie is named after him.

FAST FACT

Campbell's sheep property is now the site of the Royal Military College - Duntroon

MAKE YOUR OWN LIST

Who are three people you think are important in your family, school or suburb?

What makes a person memorable?

Garrett Cotter (1802 – 1886) Garrett Cotter was an ex-convict who was banished to live by himself beyond the limits of European settlement because of a dispute with his employer's neighbour. He was helped by the local Aboriginal people and lived with them for about five years. The Cotter River is named after him.

Major Sites in Canberra and the ACT

These sites include buildings, structures and natural features. They are important for their beauty, rarity and historic connections.

Parliament House

Construction of Australia's new Parliament House was the largest public project undertaken since the Snowy Mountains Hydro-electric Scheme in the 1960s. Located on Capital Hill, the building is designed to function for the next 200 years.

Two curved walls divide the space, with the House of Representatives and the Senate chambers on opposite sides of the building. The green colour scheme for the Senate chamber and the red colours of the House of Representatives are reminders of the links with the British Parliament, which uses similar colours.

Old Parliament House

This was meant to be a temporary building but it was in use from 1927 until 1988. By this time, the number of politicians had more than doubled and the facilities for them and their staff were very crowded. The Museum of Australian Democracy now occupies Old Parliament House.

Royal Australian Mint

The Royal Australian Mint was opened in 1965, when it began making coins for the changeover to decimal currency in 1966. The Mint also makes coins for other countries, and produces medals and tokens, as well as special orders for private customers.

Before the Mint was opened in Canberra, Australia's coins were made in branches of the British Mint in Sydney, Melbourne and Perth.

National Gallery of Australia

The National Gallery was opened in 1982. Its extensive collection of Australian art includes over 7,500 Indigenous works. The NGA also collects Asian, Pacific, European and American art.

Black Mountain

The Telstra Tower on Black Mountain provides panoramic views across Canberra. From the lookout, Walter Burley Griffin's layout of Canberra can be seen in the distance.

The Black Mountain reserve is a haven for native plants and animals adapted to its dry sclerophyll forest environment.

Shine Dome

The Shine Dome building was opened in 1959. It is the home of the Australian Academy of Science. Radical for its time, the building was designed by Roy Grounds and is on the National Heritage List.

Tidbinbilla

Tidbinbilla Nature Reserve protects a range of native wildlife, including the shy platypus. The animal habitats at Tidbinbilla include forest, grasslands, sub-alpine and wetlands.

The Canberra Space Centre at Tidbinbilla has an exhibit about the history of Australia's role in space exploration, and visitors can see the communication dish that is a part of NASA's Deep Space Network.

Heritage Trails

These walking tracks take the visitor on a tour of the ACT's historic sites

Track 1: Ngunnawal Country
Track 2: The Limestone Plains
Track 3: Looking at Canberra
Track 4: ACT Pioneers Cemetery Track
Track 5: Gungahlin Heritage Track
Track 6: Belconnen Heritage Track
Track 7: Woden Heritage Track
Track 8: Tuggeranong Heritage Track

Flags, Symbols, Emblems and Special Days of the ACT

People living in the ACT use flags, symbols and special days to show their connection to their community. These connections include pride for the group they belong to, an interest in the history of their group or area, and wanting to join others for celebrations that bring people together.

The ACT Flag

Competitions were held in 1988 and 1992 for the design of a flag for the ACT. The chosen design features the Southern Cross and a part of Canberra's Coat of Arms.

The colours of blue, gold and white refer to the colours of the City of Canberra and of the Australian Coat of Arms.

Australian Aboriginal Flag

The Aboriginal Flag was first flown in 1971. It was designed by Elder Harold Thomas.

Yellow disc - the sun and yellow ochre

Red - the land

Black - the Aboriginal people of Australia

Special Days

Australia Day - On 26th January each year, Australians commemorate the 1788 founding of a British colony by Governor Phillip at Sydney Cove.

ANZAC Day - On 25th April each year, the ANZAC Day service and ceremony are held at the Australian War Memorial in Canberra.

NAIDOC Week - A week in July each year to celebrate the history, culture and achievements of Aboriginal and Torres Strait Islander peoples. Communities and government bodies organise events for NAIDOC Week.

Canberra Day - This holiday commemorates the naming of the site of Canberra by Lady Denman, wife of the Governor General, on 12th March, 1913.

Family and Community Day is a public holiday in the ACT held on a Monday of the third term school holidays. It was first held in 2007.

RULES FOR FLYING THESE FLAGS

- Don't fly more than one on the same pole.
- Don't fly them in the dark.
- Raise the flag to the top of the pole before lowering it to half-mast.
- Treat these flags with respect.

Symbols of the ACT

Floral Emblem - Royal Bluebell
Animal Emblem - Gang-gang Cockatoo

The Coat of Arms

The Coat of Arms design was chosen in 1928 from entries in a competition. The winning design was by C. R. Wylie. The need for a Coat of Arms came from a request for a symbol that could be used on the new ship, the HMAS Canberra.

Castle - a symbol of the importance of the city
Sword of Justice - a symbol for authority
Mace - a symbol of the power to make laws
Crown - a symbol of the monarchy
Rose - the Rose of York is a symbol for the Duke of York
Portcullis or Gate - refers to the Westminster System and British Parliament
Gum tree - a symbol for growth
Swans - symbols for the Aboriginal and European peoples
Motto - "Pro Rege, Lege et Grege" which means "For the Queen, the Law and the People"

WORD FILE

Elder - a respected Aboriginal person who is a custodian of traditional knowledge
half-mast - flying a flag halfway up the pole as a mark of respect when a community leader dies

Make Your Own Coat of Arms

Design a Coat of Arms for your family, suburb or sport group, etc.

- Use symbols that everyone will know
- Your own Coat of Arms could include drawings or pictures to tell the history of the group
- Think about where to use your Coat of Arms
- What language will you use for a motto?
- Where have you seen the ACT Coat of Arms used?

How to Find Out More
Primary and Secondary Sources

There are many ways to find out more about the ACT. You can do this using both primary and secondary sources. Websites can have a mixture of both types of sources on them.

Primary Sources

- **Interviews** - when people say what they have seen
- **Letters** - when the writer was the person experiencing the event
- **Newspapers** - when the facts are presented such as a list of prices for groceries
- **Photos** - when they have not been altered
- **Maps**
- **Old Items & Antiques**
- **News on Television** - when it shows pictures of real events
- **School Newsletters** - when they list names or dates of events
- **Videos on Youtube or Facebook** - when they show an event and have not been altered

Secondary Sources

- **Letters** - when the writer is retelling the facts that someone else told them
- **Newspapers** - when the story is told by someone who retells the facts that someone else told them
- **Photos** - when the photo has been altered
- **Songs, Poems, Stories**
- **News on Television** - when it is reported by a journalist who did not experience the events

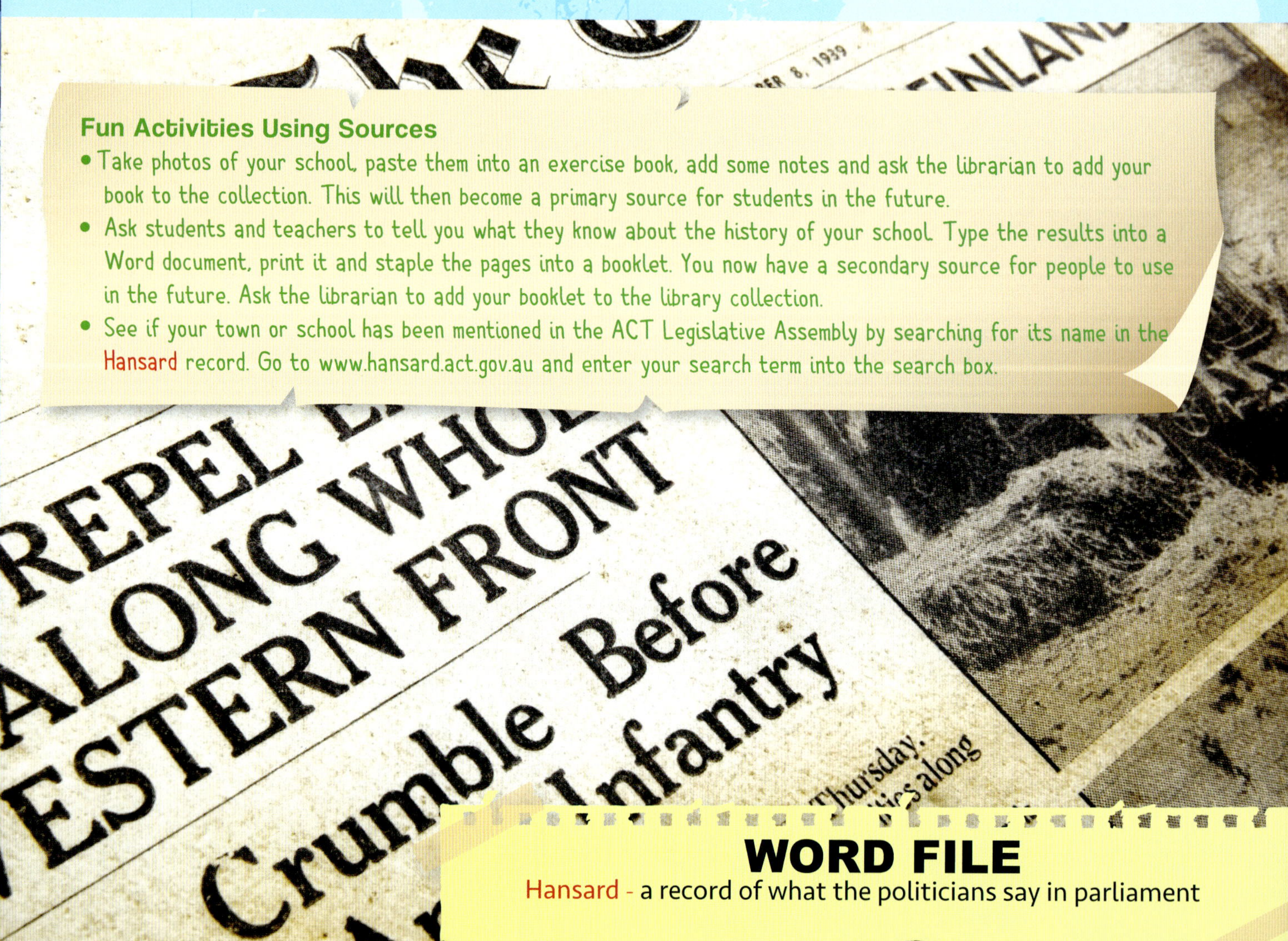

Fun Activities Using Sources

- Take photos of your school, paste them into an exercise book, add some notes and ask the librarian to add your book to the collection. This will then become a primary source for students in the future.
- Ask students and teachers to tell you what they know about the history of your school. Type the results into a Word document, print it and staple the pages into a booklet. You now have a secondary source for people to use in the future. Ask the librarian to add your booklet to the library collection.
- See if your town or school has been mentioned in the ACT Legislative Assembly by searching for its name in the Hansard record. Go to www.hansard.act.gov.au and enter your search term into the search box.

WORD FILE

Hansard - a record of what the politicians say in parliament

Your Own Family and Friends

Primary sources do not always have to be about famous people. Interviews with your family and friends are important too. Your grandmother might recall what your suburb used to be like. Friends can share stories about coming to live in Canberra and the ACT either from other states or from a country overseas.

Oldest Newspapers in the Act

The Federal Capital Pioneer was published from 1924 to 1927 and was the first newspaper in the ACT. **The Canberra Times** launched its first issue in 1926, starting as a weekly newspaper and expanding to become a daily in 1928.

NEWSPAPER OF THE ...AL CAPITAL CITY.

The Canberra Times

Mid-Week Edition.

PUBLISHED EVERY TUESDAY & FRIDAY PRICE, 3d.

No. 36 — Registered at the G.P.O., Sydney, for transmission by post as a newspaper. — CANBERRA, TUESDAY, MAY 3, 1927 — PAGES.

Busy Final Preparations For Canberra's Great Day In Australian History

...AL SERVICE.

...rangements Discussed.

...NISING STRONG POSTS

DEFENCE FORCES

Main Bodies Arrive

GREAT AIR FLEET.

The main bodies of representatives of the various units of the military, naval and aerial defence forces of the Commonwealth at the opening of Parliament House have arrived in the city, and are now under canvas in the various camps prepared by the advance parties.

The first of the main parties to arrive were the aeroplanes from Richmond (N.S.W.). They landed at the ...

Lord, and Sergt. Owen.

The Point Cook contingent did not arrive until yesterday. There were three de Haviland 9 A's, four de Haviland 9's, and three S.E.5 A's (single-seater fighters). The de Haviland 9 A's are piloted by Flight-Lieuts E. C. Wackett, W. E. C. Johnston and Sergt. L. J. Trist; the de Haviland 9's by Flight-Lieuts. D. E. L. Wilson, and W. Palstra, Flying Officer A. S. Cross, and ...

ELECTRICITY.

CHARGES REDUCED

As from May 1.

The Federal Capital Commission has effected a reduction in the charges for electric current for domestic purposes.

The reduced rates are effective as from May 1.

The new rates are 7d. per unit for lighting, and 1½d. per unit for domestic power. Power for continuous use in an electrical hot water system will be charged at ¾d. per unit.

These supersede the present charges of 9d. for light and 4d. for electric power. Necessary action is being taken for the gazettal of these rates.

Any rates payable under special bulk supply contracts will stand for the present, pending further investigation and consideration after the Royal visit. Any revision which may be made in these charges will, however, be retrospective from May 1.

DUKE'S MOUNT

MILITARY REVIEW

ROYAL PROGRESS

Duke's Tour Through City

COMPLETE ITINERA...

The complete itinerary o... of Canberra on Tuesday next ... the Duke of York, has been ... Strong posts are being f... and the following programm...

ITINERA...

MORNIN...

Inspection of South...

10.30 a.m. Leave Government ...

10.35 a.m. Mountain Way (Opp... Westridge strong p...

10.38 a.m. Cr. Adelaide Aven... lake strong post.

10.43 a.m. Cr. Continent Cir... Tree planting by ...

10.58 a.m. Cr. Wellington A... fordia strong pos...

11.2 a.m. J. B. Young's c...

11.3 a.m. Interlake Aven... Causeway str...

11.10 a.m. Federal Avenue and Capitol Circuit. ... planting by H.R.H. Duke of York.

11.30 a.m. Parliament House. Public reception.

AFTERNOON.

Inspection of Northern Districts.

3.45 p.m. Duntroon. H.R.H. Duke of York leaves Duntroon.

CANBERRA BAND.

BUSY PROGRAMME.

A meeting of the Acton branch of the Canberra Mothercraft Society was held yesterday evening, when final preparations were made for the branch's participation in Canberra's "Baby Week" during the celebrations ...

FAST FACTS

Find old newspapers at your local library. Use these to look at pictures of areas you know and to see how they have changed over time.

Primary Sources in the National Museum of Australia

The National Museum of Australia in Canberra has a collection of historic objects that belonged to explorers. Try to visit this museum and look at the objects listed below.

Captain James Cook - tea cup and magnifier
Burke and Wills - leather water bottle and copy of a hand-drawn map of their journey
Gregory Blaxland - family clock

What do these primary sources tell you about their owners?

Websites

Find more information about Canberra and the ACT on these websites:

- www.nationalcapital.gov.au
- www.ngunawal.com.au
- www.act.gov.au
- www.canberrahistory.org.au
- www.parliament.act.gov.au

Glossary

bicameral - a government having two houses or sections
colonise - to settle in a new land and impose a new culture on the people living there
Elder - a respected Aboriginal person who is a custodian of traditional knowledge
half-mast - flying a flag halfway up the pole as a mark of respect when a community leader dies
Hansard - a record of what the politicians say in parliament
precinct - an area within a city
sclerophyll forest - trees having tough leaves that resist drying out
sub-alpine - at the lower regions of mountains
sustainability - ability of the environment to be used without being destroyed
traditional ownership - the Aboriginal land ownership system in existence before the arrival of Europeans
unicameral - a government having one house or section

Index

www.redbackpublishing.com.au